Katharina Fritsch

Dia Center for the Arts, New York   April 1993–April 1994

Foreword

Katharina Fritsch conceived of <u>Rattenkönig</u> (Rat-King) following her first visit to New York at our invitation in the fall of 1989. She asked that we include in the catalogue Giorgio de Chirico's account of his first experience of New York; without doubt, in the background of the developing concepts of <u>Rattenkönig</u> lies the shock of a foreign culture and this looming urban environment. I can put this source of inspiration in a positive light at least insofar as I believe that <u>Rattenkönig</u> is Fritsch's most powerful work to date.

The piece lays out in a perfect circle, defined in a macabre geometry, by sixteen black rats of larger-than-human scale, pulling with equal force from a central point: the knot in their tails that is common to and paralyzes them all. The rats are clones of Fritsch's <u>Ur-Rat</u>: a distilled, essential rat form first sculpted in plaster, then reproduced in a silicon mold. Their matte blackness comes from within—a marriage of the ideas of Rat and Knot with the color black. In the modeling, Fritsch avoided overly naturalistic detail where it could render the imagery too particular, at remove from an archetype (of Rat or Knot) we could all recognize.

One of Fritsch's great contributions is her classical emphasis on clear form in art. Visual clarity is primary for Fritsch, and the figuration in <u>Rattenkönig</u> is, like much of her work, sharply focused. This contributes to the breathtaking immediacy of the work. Your eye takes in the forms in an instant. In addition, further accelerating the impact of the work on the senses, there is a totemic quality to her imagery; it has an archetypal directness.

Fritsch's highly ordered formal vision is at odds with the deep emotional content of the work. In <u>Rattenkönig</u>, the clearly articulated forms struggle energetically with things felt but unseen. The tension between the visible and the invisible heightens our faculties of perception and imagination. This is uplifting, as the perception of an essence is uplifting, notwithstanding the darker, unsettling references of Rat, Knot, and Rat-King.

In <u>Rattenkönig</u>, the rats struggle to become individuated, tightening the knot that binds them to a familial hell. A condition from which there is no exit, or the absolute loss of the force of will, is a theme repeated in different terms in other earlier works represented in this catalogue: <u>Mann und Maus</u> (Man and Mouse), 1991, and <u>Tischgesellschaft</u> (Company at Table), 1988. These three works are not part of a series, but they examine, in part, the same existential nightmare.

It is rare when an artist's most ambitious work is also her most successful. <u>Rattenkönig</u> achieves this and suggests that Fritsch has reached a new height.

Charles Wright, Executive Director

Parerga

I

Rodents: the very sound of the word engenders a hyper-inflated response. Rats, mice, voles … are automatically and inescapably associated with dirt, disease, and death. Doubtless, certain of their attributes contribute to their bad reputation. For example, not only do rats have cannibalistic tendencies, but when under attack, they display an unbridled aggression that leads them to leap, bite, then hang by their teeth wherever they land. Rodents, like humans, are not highly specialized animals and thus are more adaptable than most: their ubiquity is proverbial.

Predating scientific understanding of the intersection of germs, contamination, illness, and mortality, their seemingly inevitable association with negative and malign forces is hence both deep-rooted and irrational. But it is not only as vermin—another loaded word, and one with an appropriately onomatopoeic vividness—that these creatures instill disgust and fear: perhaps even more effective in fanning the flames of antipathy than their actual behavior are their exploits, as recounted in a plethora of legends and myths, travelogues, and other literary accounts, and as depicted in numerous illustrations ranging from populist broadsides to emblemata.[1] Since medieval times at least, rats have served as metaphors for the demonic and horrific, an association that continues to have great currency, as witnessed, for example in F. W. Murnau's Nosferatu (1921), in which the principal protagonist resembles a rat; and in the most recent Batman film, Batman Returns (1992), in which the villainous Penguin also has rodentlike features. In literature they display an equal longevity and vitality—witness Albert Camus's classic The Plague (1948) and Günter Grass's recent novel The Rat (1986).

That the freakish and the horrific cohabit is a prevalent idea in the collective imaginary, one which numerous writers have capitalized on, possibly none better than Edgar Allan Poe in his brilliant, chilling tale "The Pit and the Pendulum," in which rats are at once the source of greatest dread and the means of escape. But rats themselves may be the subject of unnatural occurrence, as evidenced in the rat-king. Various claims have been advanced concerning the origins of this strange phenomenon in which a number of rats become bound together by the inextricable knotting of their tails.[2] Those that assert that the animals were born this way are now largely discredited, as are those that maintain that their own community feeds them and accords them a central role reminiscent of that played by the queen bee in a hive. More recent and more sound scholarship argues that the phenomenon arises serendipitously among young rats, which when playing together in a nest, or even when cleaning themselves, may become enmeshed if suddenly disturbed. Once inescapably bound together, their prospects of survival are limited since they depend on the scraps left by the larger community to which they belong. Frequently, however, they are discovered on account of their shrill squealing before they perish.

While the rat-king has an impressive literary and visual pedigree, verified sightings are relatively few and, curiously, limited principally to Germany, which may account not only for the original coining of the term in that language but for the continuing place the concept has in that nation's popular imagination.

II

Rattenkönig (Rat-King) is the third in a trio of sculptures Katharina Fritsch has made in recent years that she feels deals with the dark side of the psyche.[3] The other two are Tischgesellschaft (Company at Table), 1988, and Mann und Maus (Man and Mouse), 1992. In the earliest of these, the disconcerting, even disturbing, effect depends on the seemingly endless repetition of the same male figure seated morosely at a long table. Here, anomie is evoked through symbolic rather than didactic or illustrative language. Not only do the inertness of the figure, oblivious to all outside himself, and the blankness of his physiognomy contribute to quasi-catatonia, but equally crucial is the formalization—the stylization and simplification—which makes him more generic than individual in type. Moreover, repetition is taken to a point beyond easy assimilation, so that it begins to appear at once redundant and excessive, and almost unbearable. Furthermore, the endless circular pattern in the specially designed tablecloth, together with the stringently delimited palette of red, white, and black, similarly reinforce the effect of strict formal supervision, lifting the image out of the realm of sociohistorical critique and into the metaphysical.

<u>Mann und Maus</u>, executed four years later, employs the same male model. The figure now lies in bed, the covers drawn up to his chin. A giant black mouse perches brazenly on his chest. Each stares straight ahead: the human figure as if transfixed, the animal apparently impervious. Momentarily humorous in its horribleness, the image ultimately derives its potency from drawing on a source long known but long unacknowledged. That is, it seems to tap into some collective cultural memory to which one has immediate access though not necessarily via personal experience. A deep-seated recognition coupled with an unsettling sense of unexpectedness ensue, as if that which is most abhorrent has invaded the central realms of the psyche without its knowledge. That the image is capable of interweaving fears of infiltration, possession, violation, and other nameless, but fundamental forms of dread, depends on its formulaic character. Having standardized this quotidian trope, Fritsch then infuses it with a vivid quiddity and a visceral richness that together heighten the effect of immutable presence. The resulting "indefinite definiteness," to borrow Poe's apt term, proves essential to the epiphanic encounter. Indeed, among this subject's many antecedents may be found Poe's own bewitched black cat, which also bore implacably on the breast of its assailant, and, more distantly, Henri Fuseli's homunculus astride a prostrate maiden. Once the fantastic is somehow rendered "natural," the macabre can settle into the mind, governing it with an inexorable, if dreadful, logic.

Fritsch conceived <u>Rattenkönig</u> after hearing about the phenomenon from a friend. As he recounted the details, she had the feeling that she had already known of it but had somehow suppressed or forgotten the information: the retelling became a kind of reminding. A similar effect of recall may be initially experienced by the viewer on first encounter, though arguably this image itself will ultimately become indelibly branded in the viewer's psyche. In the handling of scale, proportion, and form, <u>Rattenkönig</u> manifests a similar fastidiousness to that which informs both <u>Tischgesellschaft</u> and <u>Mann und Maus</u>. Symmetry, clarity, and an astutely calibrated proportion and scale again help wed fixation to presence. And as before, the elements are generic in character, and so, once more, indefiniteness is counterpointed with the specificity integral to an hallucinatory effect.

Crouching in a tight ring, their heads thrust forward ominously toward the spectator, their tails streaming behind them, the rats' bodies are composed into a strong abstract shape resembling the spokes of a wheel. If the pure geometry of their configuration metaphorically symbolizes both their regimentation and their incarceration in this hellish trap, the knot, the source of their misfortune, at once attenuates and underscores this effect. Highly stylized and hence even more abstract in form than the bodies of the rodents, it appears a pure node at the center of the composition. By means of the lucid and fluent weaving together of the skeins of tails, the knot becomes a point of stasis and resolution rather than of potential chaos and implosion. Although barely glimpsed between the haunches of the huge forms, it nonetheless crucially contributes to the metamorphosis of this phenomenon from the simply abhorrent into an image replete with grandeur and monumentality, a wonder, as distinct from merely a freak of nature.

After closely studying taxidermists' specimens as well as photographs of live rats, Fritsch began to build up the final form by fusing characteristics taken from members of both the brown and the black species, irrespective of the fact that from the beginning she had decided that black must be the color of her animals. Experiments with different numbers soon revealed that sixteen rats were required to compose a ring of sufficient magnitude to encircle the two freestanding columns in the Dia space, where the work was to have its debut. In general, Fritsch prefers four and its multiples—4, 8, 16, 32…—because she feels that these numbers have a formal completeness and resolution, a symmetry, balance, and immutable equilibrium not offered by other integers. While not determining her thinking, number symbolism nevertheless informs a reasoning based primarily in formal considerations.[4]

The gestation of this piece was relatively brief; however, its realization, as is customary with Fritsch's mode of working, proved painstaking and protracted. Her attempts to make of the art object an equivalent for a long-past but cherished experience frequently involve her in complicated negotiations, elaborate research, and typically relentless editing in order to approximate those mnemonic traces and echoes she so treasures. Although the touchstone of the rightness of the realization is always the artist's feelings, the results are far from expressionist in either style or form. Since artifice, distillation, and a fastidious refining are her principal tools, there is never evidence of her hand in the final piece and little that an unsuspecting observer might identify as autobiographical in tenor. "I don't aim for expressiveness," she states. "That is a concept that I find too spongy, too vague. On the contrary, I find precision to be the best possible contribution one can make to … show … the clarity of the things themselves—the essential qualities and characteristics."[5]

Whether of pencil cases or wallpaper patterns, the once personal memories Fritsch seeks to salvage are to her no different in principle from those motifs she derives from collective culture and which form the basis for other works: the Madonna, the man and mouse, the elephant, or the rat-king. All are "autobiographical and at the same time … carry a level of significance that is generally understandable," she contends.[6] When arrayed in a green coat, an elephant modeled from a specimen in a natural history museum display turns into an object of wonder. Comparable to Dürer's rhinoceros, which has continued for centuries to fascinate artists and others even though long known to be far from an accurate portrayal, it is also akin to those earnest renderings of beached whales made by enthralled seventeenth-century Dutch draftsmen, which still today captivate the imagination.[7] Repeatedly in Western art, the marvels of nature made visible initially through the power of an artist's vision themselves become works of art and then, in turn, develop their own trajectories as objects of curiosity and wonder.

Phantoms and apparitions, which are equally haunting to the human imaginary, often prove to be cousins to these "natural" wonders: <u>Madonna</u>, based on a souvenir from the pilgrimage center at Lourdes, becomes an idol pure and simple when coated a hallucinatory yellow. But irrespective of whether fantastic or religious in derivation—whether a Madonna or a ghost and pool of blood, for instance—they all have what Julian Heynen so aptly calls "the simultaneous embeddedness and distance of a symbolically overworked image." Consequently, in Fritsch's appropriation of them, as he astutely contends, "The hackneyed, [the] all-too-familiar, … is tested for its core of collective credibility and placed in a new, contemporary context."[8]

The majority of these resonant moments—memories, fantasies, and other lingering visions—are rendered in Fritsch's oeuvre as three-dimensional form, but on occasion she has utilized the ephemeral to evoke itself. Perfume lingering in a hallway, the (recorded) sound of rain pervading a domestic room stenciled with the artist's own wallpaper pattern, or the haunting whistle of wind in a chimney, barely audible in a stately room whose walls have been rendered a sumptuous deep red, are among this group of immaterial works.[9] Also allied to these evocations is her plan (so far unrealized) to have a black truck with a red load drive endlessly throughout Germany. This proposal can be compared with the project she devised in 1986 for <u>Sonsbeek</u> in which an elderly man strolled with his dog through part of the exhibition site, a landscaped park. A postcard of the protagonists was made as a souvenir. For technical reasons the performance was only held once, however knowledge of it spread so effectively that many people were convinced they had actually witnessed the promenade, even though that could not have been the case. As with the truck, the possibility that one might have glimpsed it, or that one might happen upon it in the future, becomes as potent as was the prospect of the imminent arrival of the <u>Flying Dutchman</u> to a previous era. For these tropes function similarly: like rumor, they are quickly ignited and highly contagious, often ending in a form of collective hysteria. Given their compelling plausibility, they might be deemed plebeian visitations.

Fritsch's images are often culled from the vernacular—collective phobias, superstition, or folklore—rather than from the realm of high art, because, as Proust well knew, in high art affectivity tends to fall victim to the immutability of the masterwork. Theodor Adorno convincingly argues of the French writer that "…nothing has substance for him but what has already been mediated by memory," concluding that "his love dwells on the second life [the afterlife, of posterity], the one which is already over, rather than on the first." And he continues in terms that, again, apply equally well to Fritsch: "For Proust's aestheticism the question of aesthetic quality is of secondary concern. In a famous passage he glorified inferior music for the sake of the listener's memories, which are preserved with far more fidelity and force in an old popular song than in the self-sufficiency of a work by Beethoven."[10] Yet ultimately the question of their pedigree in either high art or mass culture becomes irrelevant for, as Adorno noted, distinctions between different levels of culture are eliminated once they are no longer isolated as domains of the objective mind and are drawn into the stream of subjectivity. In order to act as madeleines, the objects Fritsch produces must be carefully constructed artifacts. Designed to act as catalysts, they cannot be the things themselves, unlike fetishes and relics. Likewise, their singularity has little to do with notions of uniqueness. Just as the dream image and memory-fragment create a simulacrum of the initial stimulant, these works take on hybrid identities, being strictly speaking neither original nor copy.

Although much has been made of the fact that Fritsch produces serial forms and uses techniques that relate to mass production and industrial fabrication, what is at stake is less a matter of collapsing distinctions between artworks and mundane artifacts than one of utilizing techniques that allow for replication and duplication. In the past, certain sculptors employed casting processes to related ends, as seen in the practice of Rodin who, for example, placed three identical casts of a figure derived from his sculpture known as Adam atop the Gates of Hell, baptizing them The Three Shades. On numerous other occasions he duplicated, modified, and recombined aspects of the same or related figures to create new composite or hybrid wholes.[11]

Fritsch's recent monumental pieces contrast with many of the smaller sculptures and the multiples from the beginning of her career, a number of which she has presented on pedestals constructed to resemble merchandise racks.[12] Almost all, including the sheep, small yellow Madonnas, black cats, beads, various vehicles, plus the tiny grey mill, have the character of toys, knick-knacks, souvenirs, or items from Nativity crèches.[13] As miniatures they might be said to have a surrogate existence: they belong to a hypothetical realm, one that lies outside the functional and diurnal. Their size, coupled with the fact that they look mass-produced, means that they cannot readily be linked directly to a fine-art tradition. Their identity remains highly ambiguous—not quite estranged from ordinary life yet, given both their appearance and mode of presentation, existing apart from the ordinary. What is undeniable, however, is that though works of art, they simultaneously inhabit the realm of common culture and collective biography.

In an essay adumbrating a philosophy of toys, Charles Baudelaire wrote: "The toy is the child's earliest initiation to art, or rather for him it is the first concrete example of art, and when mature age comes, the perfected examples will not give his mind the same feelings of warmth, nor the same enthusiasms, nor the same sense of conviction."[14] For Bruno Bettelheim, fairy tales play a comparable role: they are a crucial point of entry into high culture, since they are "works of art which are fully comprehensible to the child, as no other form of art is."[15] These somewhat contending claims may be reconciled by accepting Susan Stewart's argument that the "toy is the physical embodiment of the fiction: it is a device for fantasy, a point of beginning for narrative. The toy opens an interior world, lending itself to fantasy and privacy in a way that the abstract space, the playground, of social play does not."[16] Toys constitute a particular subset within the category of the miniature, which inhabits the infinite time of reverie, an other time which negates change and the flux of lived reality. This compressed time of interiority, she contends in a fascinating study of the subject, transcends the duration of everyday life, creating an island that remains perfect and pristine. In short, "it is linked to nostalgic versions of childhood and history, present[ing] a diminutive, and thereby manipulatable, version of experience, a version which is domesticated and protected from contamination."[17] If the miniature is found "at the origin of private, individual history," its antithesis, the gigantic, has the public and natural history as its initial frame of reference.[18] Both provide analogical modes of thought: the miniature, the mental world of proportion, control, and balance; the gigantic, a world of disorder, grotesquerie, profanity, and licentiousness—the uncontrollable, the eruptive, and the invasive.

In her work, Fritsch seeks to engender the immediate affectivity and ineffability integral to childhood experience but only seldom recaptured after, as in unexpected, unparalleled moments of wonder. It is appropriate that the means she adopts resemble those inherent in such initiatory works of art as toys and fairy tales (as defined by Baudelaire and Bettelheim respectively). In the case of her miniature sculptures, the epiphany is conjured by those feelings of intimacy and interiority particular to toys, souvenirs, and keepsakes; with the monumental pieces it is galvanized by feelings traditionally associated with the sublime—terror and awe.[19]

The classic fairy tale makes it appear that everyone is part of a universal community marked by shared values and norms and a collective striving for the same happiness; that there are dreams and wishes that are irrefutable; and that particular types of behavior will produce certain guaranteed results. Given their recurrent themes, stock types, and repetitive patterns, together with their bold divisions of the world into polarities of black and white, or good and evil, the formulaic structures and subcategories of the tale types are readily identifiable. Given that they have been deemed critical to the socialization of the child and fundamental to interpreting the psychological needs and drives of the individual as well as the collective wisdom of a culture, their function is akin to that of classical and other myths. For Roland Barthes, myth is a collective representation that is socially determined and then inverted, in such a way that it loses its appearance as a cultural artifact. "Myth consists in overturning culture into nature," he writes, "or, at least, the social, the cultural, the ideological, the historical into the 'natural' …. [U]nder the effect of mythical inversion, the quite contingent foundations of the utterance become Common Sense, Right Reason, the Norm, General Opinion, in short the doxa (which is the secular figure of the Origin)."[20] According to Barthes, traditional myths and their affiliates may easily become contemporary myths and so may continue to permeate and regulate everyday life.

German fairy tales and folk tales—Märchen—collectively constitute a literary form largely created by the Grimm brothers as they continually refined and "improved" the texts they collected.[21] Their corpus has become a shared national property: Kinder- und Hausmärchen is the most widely reprinted and translated book in Germany after the Bible. The Urmärchen, the parent tales, if they ever existed, can no longer be recovered; however, as a result of the Grimms' retrieval and preservation, since their time, folklore has been considered a part of the nation's cultural treasury. Regarding them as far from exclusive to the province of childhood, for over a century the Germans have, as Jack Zipes argues, "repeatedly used fairy tales to explain the world to themselves."[22] In addition to cultivating ancient folk tales, they have also developed the most remarkable literary fairy-tale tradition in the West. For almost all significant German (including Swiss and Austrian) writers from the mid-nineteenth century to the present have either written or endeavored to write a fairy tale, and many philosophers and critics, including Ernst Bloch and Walter Benjamin, have analyzed them. Thus in Germany more than elsewhere, Zipes contends, the Märchen have become "a sacred convention and [are] used as … a metaphorical medium to attain truth…."[23] In the post–World War II era, they have continued, notwithstanding their association with the völkisch and their appropriation in part by the Nazis, to be "used widely in the schools in a spiritualist, religious, and aesthetic manner that downplayed [their] historical and social significance … and stressed their 'marvelous,' therapeutic, and mystical qualities."[24]

Elias Canetti once contended that "a more accurate study of fairy tales would teach us what we can still expect of the world"[25]—a high regard for the Märchen that echoes Friedrich Schiller's avowal made over a hundred years earlier that "Deeper meaning resides in the fairy tales told to me in my childhood than in the truth that is taught by life."[26] These statements have taken on the guise of conventional wisdom and might easily be assented to by Fritsch—albeit with significant qualifications. Fritsch became enthralled by myths, fables, Märchen, and biblical stories at an early and impressionable age. In continuing to inform her memories of childhood, they permeated her aesthetic: in formal terms, in her preference for a symbolic discourse; and in her perception of the role of the work of art. Yet, like many of her contemporaries, including Grass, she does not fully endorse the values and ideals they encode, but renders them ambivalent when not partially inverting them.

By manifesting a preference for this vehicle as a mode of apprehending truth, contemporary artists might be thought to have implicitly rejected scientific and secular rationality. Yet such need not be the case, as Hans Blumenberg argues in his impressive and momentous study of the role of myth.[27] Investigating why, with the triumphant advance of science and of Enlightenment ideals, the old myths have not simply withered and evaporated, he challenges what he regards as false alternatives. On the one hand, most current interpretations of science remain within the Enlightenment tradition, implying a role for myth in the modern age that is restricted exclusively to the aesthetic imagination and assumed to have no bearing on the preeminent role of scientific rationality in our sensuous, practical lives. The counter-position is the quintessentially Romantic one, which interprets the survival of myth as evidence of it being inherent in human nature, and even, given its seemingly greater antiquity and ubiquity, of it being more fundamental to human nature than our "surface" rationality.[28]

Rejecting these well-rehearsed positions, Blumenberg focuses instead on the problem that myth seeks to solve, which is, for him, its source of real and lasting importance—namely, to contend with what he deems "the absolutism of reality." In its manifold guises, myth for him attempts to address the intense fear and dread lacking an unambiguous cause or a specific threat that permeates human existence. Thus the role of myth, he argues, is to forestall the angst that that problem produces by rationalizing it into plain fear of specific named agencies, more or less personalized powers that can be addressed and to such an extent dealt with. Both in the history of the species, and in the development of individuals, there is probably no point of demarcation, Blumenberg contends, when rationality takes over (or should take over) completely from more "childish," "prerational" modes of thought involving, for example, fantasy. Indeed, "flight behind an image," a phrase used by Goethe to describe one of his own characteristic procedures, may be a necessary recourse at any age in the face of issues that rationality cannot yet, or perhaps cannot ever, handle. An example of the latter may be the issue of self-knowledge and identity, in which the element of irreducibly "brute" inheritance may be, for the individual, an "absolute reality," in the sense that a conceptual grasp of it does not even potentially enable one to change. In this case, it may be that the quasi-mythical patterns that Freud found in dreams and elsewhere can partake of the same functional legitimacy as Goethe's "images," though this does not require regarding them as eternal, cosmic "givens" in the manner of, for example, Carl Jung. Nor does it necessitate that the functioning of the images must or even can be naive and unreflected. As Blumenberg says, myth is only known in and through our "work" on it—an expression that intentionally avoids distinguishing between imaginative and conceptual-analytical work. For he argues that from the very beginning of recorded tradition, humankind's dealings with myth have been self-conscious, "commenting on" it (as in Homer's ironical humor about the gods) while handing it on. This does not, of course, prevent its images from functioning affectively in everyday life.

Thus, from Blumenberg's perspective, the literary treatment of myth cannot be segregated as a "merely aesthetic" matter with no bearing on the practical business of life. On the other hand, literature and the visual arts will not derive their potency from a "given" stock of mythical images received from the preliterate strata of consciousness or history, and merely repackaged. Recycled through contemporary culture in art, film, and literature, mythic images and their relatives in the <u>Märchen</u>, biblical tales, and other ancient fables are continually made anew. In drawing on them for their principal subject matter, contemporary artists are not necessarily constrained to create works which are the products of quietist, regressive thinking, and <u>Innerlichkeit</u>, as is demonstrated by Fritsch and certain of her peers.

Lynne Cooke

Notes

1. For a fuller discussion, see Marten Hart, <u>Rats</u> (London: Alison and Busby, 1973).
2. See K. Becker & H. Kemper, <u>Der Rattenkönig</u> (Berlin: Duncker & Humblot, 1964). By contrast the Mouse King, a seven-headed animal with a single body and the villain in a story by E.T.A. Hoffmann ("The Nutcracker and the Mouse King"), and later in the ballet, <u>The Nutcracker</u>, seems to be a purely imaginary phenomenon.
3. This and others of Fritsch's opinions found in this essay were expressed in discussions with the author during the spring of 1993.
4. Every rat occupies one of the cardinal points of the compass. Quite different is <u>Charms</u>, 1986, a vitrine containing on each of the glass panes of its long sides thirteen small black images of chimney sweeps. In Germany, good luck is said to spring from espying a chimney sweep and then rubbing a small metal object like a button. The decision to use thirteen motifs per pane accords with the superstition underpinning the imagery.
5. "Katharina Fritsch interviewed by Marie Luise Syring & Christiane Vielhaber," <u>BiNATIONALE: German Art of the Late '80s</u> (Düsseldorf: Städtische Kunsthalle, 1988), 117.
6. Ibid., 116.
7. For an account of responses to Dürer's woodcut of the rhinoceros, refer to Colin Eisler, <u>Dürer's Animals</u> (Washington, D.C.: Smithsonian Institute Press, 1991) 269–274. For accounts and drawings of beached whales, refer to Simon Schama, <u>The Embarrassment of Riches: An Interpretation of Dutch Culture in the Golden Age</u> (New York: Alfred A. Knopf, 1987), 130–150.
8. Julian Heynen, "Speculations on Trucks, Cemeteries, Foxes and Other Images," <u>Parkett</u>, no. 25 (1990), 54.
9. The sound components from several of the installations were separately issued as records: <u>Regen</u> (Rain), 1987; <u>Unken</u> (Toads), 1982/88, 2nd edition 1990; <u>Mühle</u> (Mill), 1990; <u>Krankenwagen</u> (Ambulance), 1990.
10. Theodor Adorno, "Valéry Proust Museum," <u>Prisms</u> (Cambridge, Mass.: The MIT Press, 1981), 182.
11. For a discussion of Rodin's working methods, including the transformation of <u>Adam</u> into the figure that became known as <u>The Shade</u> see Albert E. Elsen, <u>The Gates of Hell by Auguste Rodin</u> (Stanford: Stanford University Press, 1985), 83.
12. When constructing a large work from numerous smaller items, as in the columns of vases or Madonnas, Fritsch is concerned both with notions of abundance as it shades off into excess and with the hallucinatory effect made by a monument comprised of multiple versions of the same item.
13. Although some have served as prototypes or models for works that were later realized on a grand scale, such as the functioning water mill, this is not their primary role, and so they must be seen in company with others of a similar size.
14. Charles Baudelaire, "A Philosophy of Toys," <u>The Painter of Modern Life and Other Essays</u> (London: Phaidon, 1964), 199. Interestingly, Baudelaire uses as his example of a toy belonging to a poor child a live rat that the infant's parents had caged for him.
15. Bruno Bettelheim, <u>The Uses of Enchantment: The Meaning and Importance of Fairy Tales</u> (New York: Alfred A. Knopf, 1976), 12.
16. Susan Stewart, <u>On Longing: Narratives of the Miniature, the Gigantic, the Souvenir, the Collection</u> (Baltimore: The Johns Hopkins University Press, 1984), 56.
17. Ibid., 69.
18. Ibid., 71.
19. This discussion of the miniature and monumental sculptures ignores a whole group of "life-size" works in Fritsch's oeuvre, which belong to the realm of household goods and furniture (as well as the projects for public works, notably the cemeteries, parks, and tennis court). Based on the assumption that the objects that make up one's environment influence one's attitudes and values, this group of works proposes models on which new standards may be built. In her search for a standardized, uncompromising beauty in these objects and in her regard for childhood phenomena and mnemonic fragments, Fritsch's aesthetic may be compared with that of the German poet Stefan George (1868–1933), whose work she much admires. A highly self-conscious and deliberate poet, George assimilated ideas of dedication and discipline into aestheticism, and in his art, will and intention were manifestly at work in the process of composition. His aesthetic places great stress on form, formal precision, and concision; on impression in preference to entertainment; and on the poem as less the reproduction of a thought than of a mood. Cultural renewal lies ultimately at the heart of George's ambitions: he

praised Nietzsche for proclaiming the end of an old era, but pitied him for his failure to formulate and put into practice the way in which the new was to be brought about. Fritsch's interest in Nietzsche, one of the few philosophers she is drawn to, is remarkably similar.

20. Roland Barthes, "Change the Object Itself: Mythology Today," Image—Music—Text (New York: Hill & Wang, 1977), 165.

21. The most resilient genre in German literary history since the eighteenth-century, Märchen is a comprehensive term comprising folk and fairy tales, legends, fables, anecdotes, didactic narratives, and journeymen's tales, all of which were transformed into literary products by the Grimms and others from the educated classes.

22. Jack Zipes, The Brothers Grimm: From Enchanted Forests to the Modern World (London: Routledge, 1988), 75.

23. Ibid., 87.

24. Ibid., 94.

25. Elias Canetti, The Human Province (New York: The Seabury Press, 1978), 33.

26. Friedrich Schiller, The Piccolominis III, 4 (Boston: F. A. Niccolls & Co., 1902).

27. Hans Blumenberg, Work on Myth (Cambridge: The MIT Press, 1985).

28. I am heavily indebted to the "Translator's Introduction" by Robert M. Wallace for this exposition of Blumenberg's thesis.

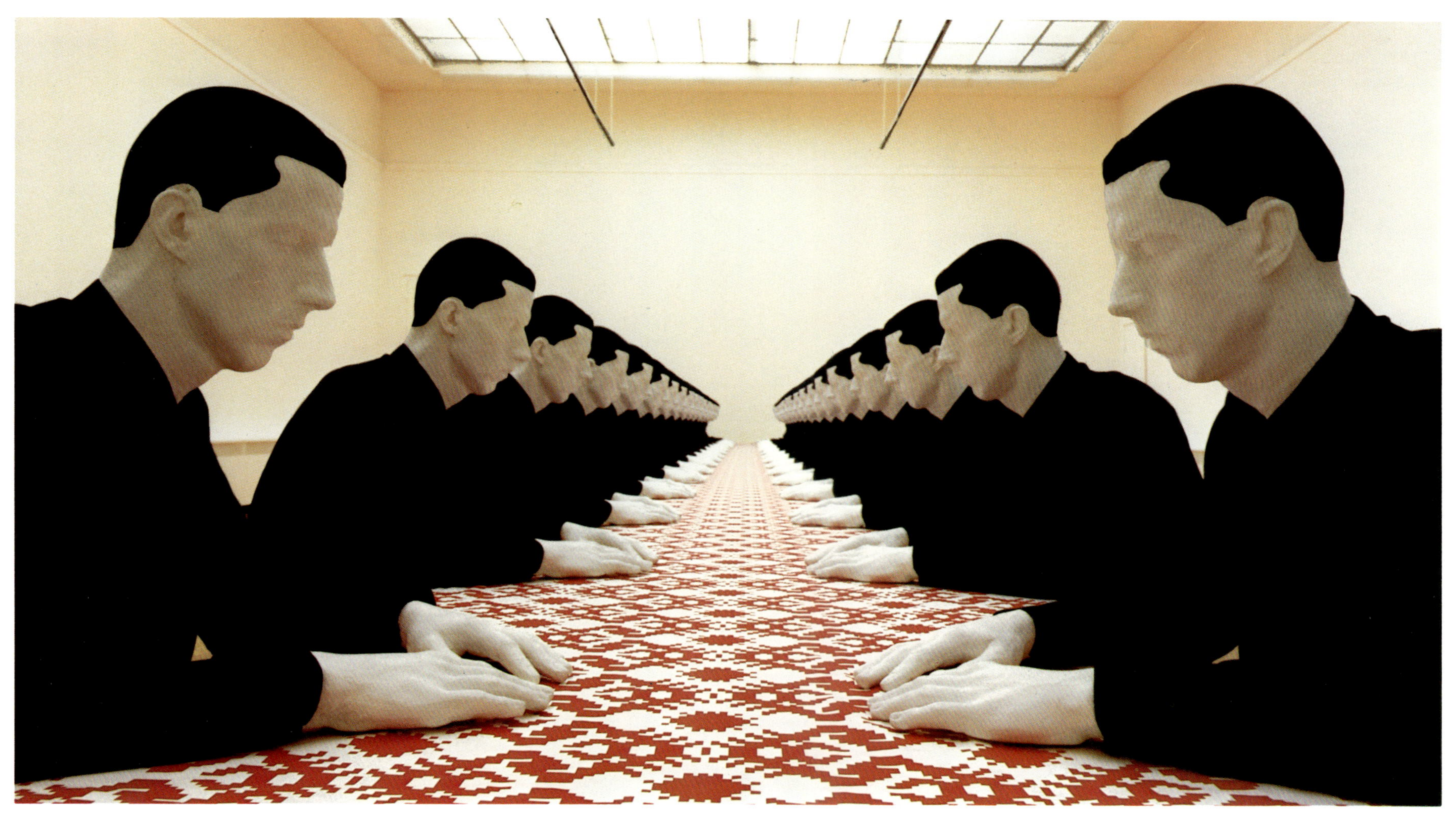

Tischgesellschaft
1988, Polyester, wood, and cotton, 55 x 630 x 69 inches

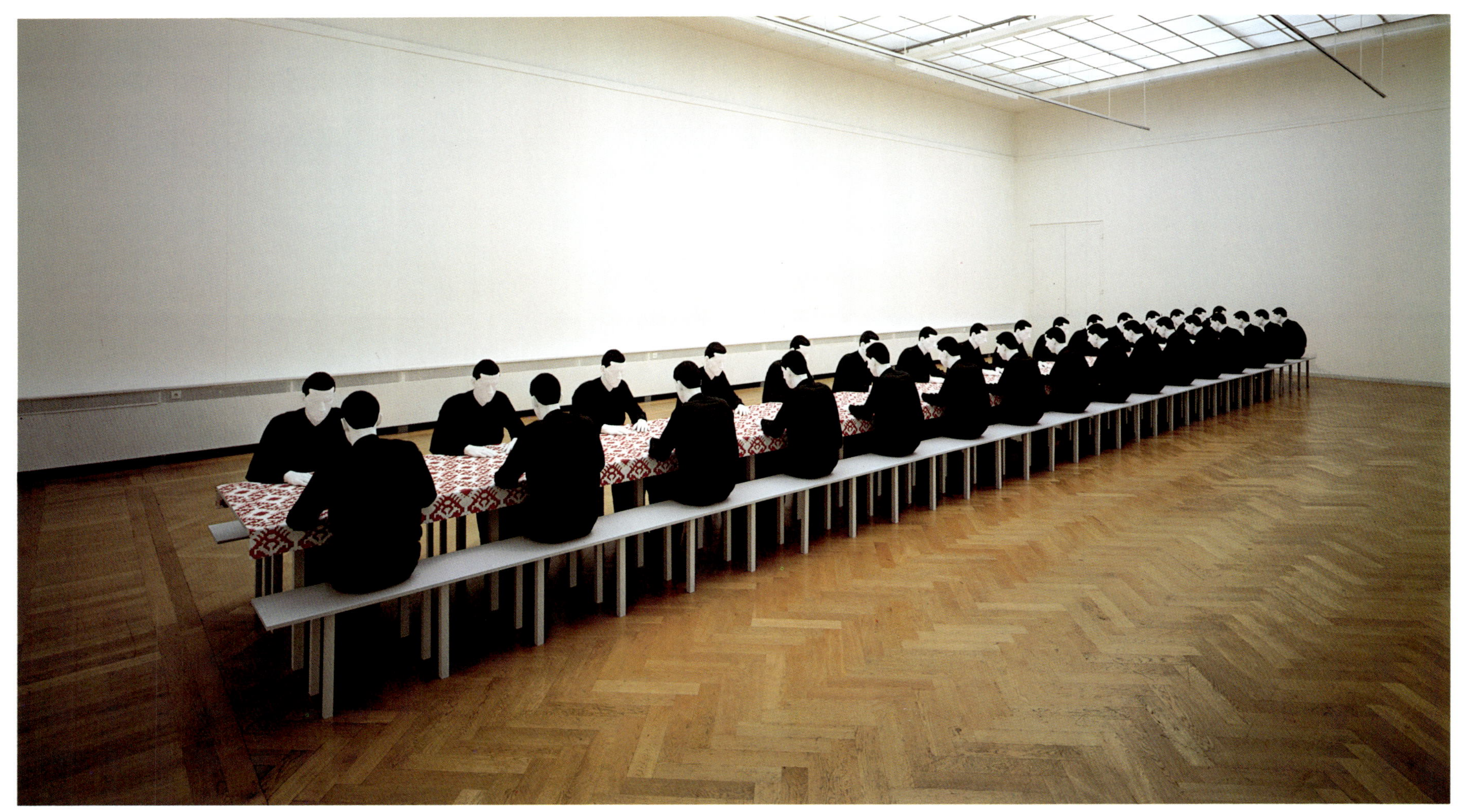

Tischgesellschaft
1988, Polyester, wood, and cotton, 55 x 630 x 69 inches

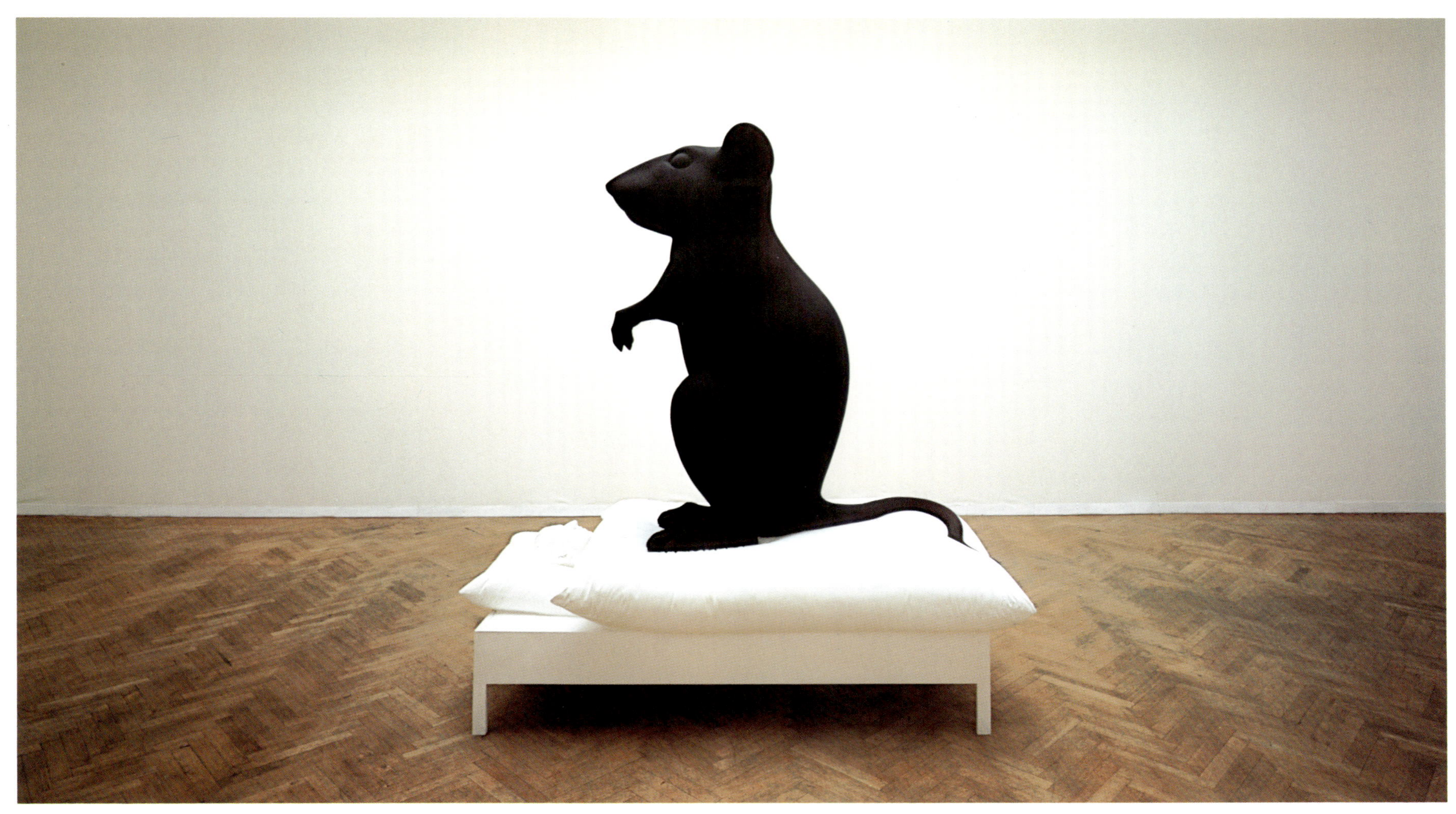

Mann und Maus
1992, Polyester resin, 90 1/2 x 51 1/5 x 94 1/2 inches

The Rat-King: Symbol of a magical connection or a freak of nature?

Rats have long occupied people's imaginations, even feeding superstition. Both old and new books about animals describe them as greedy, nocturnal rodents that live off human garbage. People are frightened of them because of their incredible adaptability and resilience but admire them for their social behavior, their "cleverness" and their sharp sense of orientation.

Reports about the "rat-king" date back to the middle of the sixteenth century. The term is used to describe the strange phenomenon of several rats linked together, unable to free themselves. Their tails do not grow together but become intertwined, then tied, often with straw, dirt, and hairs bind them together. Usually composed from five to twelve rats, the largest known rat-king was formed from thirty-two animals.

Originating in medieval German, the term <u>Rattenkönig</u> has subsequently gained English and French equivalents: "rat-king" and "<u>roi de rats</u>" respectively. Reports about the rat-king have regularly appeared in books of zoology and natural history since the end of the Middle Ages. In their book <u>Der Rattenkönig</u> (1964), the German zoologists Becker and Kemper describe thirty-seven instances of rat-kings ranging over the past five centuries. The oldest report dates from 1564, the most recent from 1963, from Rucphen in the Netherlands. Interestingly, most were found in Germany, others have been discovered in France, Switzerland, and Java.

Examining a rat-king from a detached, scientific viewpoint reveals the following: rat-kings are formed, without exception, from black house rats only, not from the more common brown ones. This is probably due to the length of the tail. Since black rats have longer and more flexible tails the possibility of a connection is more likely. Those individuals that form a rat-king are of the same size and therefore almost the same age.

Rat-kings have usually been found alive, discovered on account of their loud squeaking. Even though they are often almost fully grown, the rats are surprisingly well nourished. Speculation that the animals in a rat-king are fed by other rats has not been proven. Since rat-kings are only able to survive among a larger group of rats (of at least one hundred individuals), they probably live on leftover food. If many rats live in a very small area and are suddenly startled while cleaning or warming each other, the abrupt dispersal might lead to a linking of their long and flexible tails.

Thus the question arises as to the duration of their linkage. Full-grown rats linked together into a king have displayed sharpened, not blunted, claws on their toes: this indicates a considerable period of time of linkage. The swelling and strangling of the tissue, leading to the dried up tail tips, also indicates a long period of being tied together. Vortex fractures in the tails in the knotted area, which can be seen on X-ray photographs, show that these probably occurred when the rats tried to free themselves.

In the past, rat-kings were also artificially formed since they were a major attraction at fairs. These could easily be distinguished from the genuine ones, however, because of the loose and regular tying of the knot. That rat-kings have fascinated people ever since they were known is attested by their presence in fables, fairy tales, and other stories. A medieval image has been found, showing a knot of tails forming a throne for the king rat, who sits there while holding court.

Prof. Dr. Christian Winter
Zoologisches Institut, Frankfurt am Main

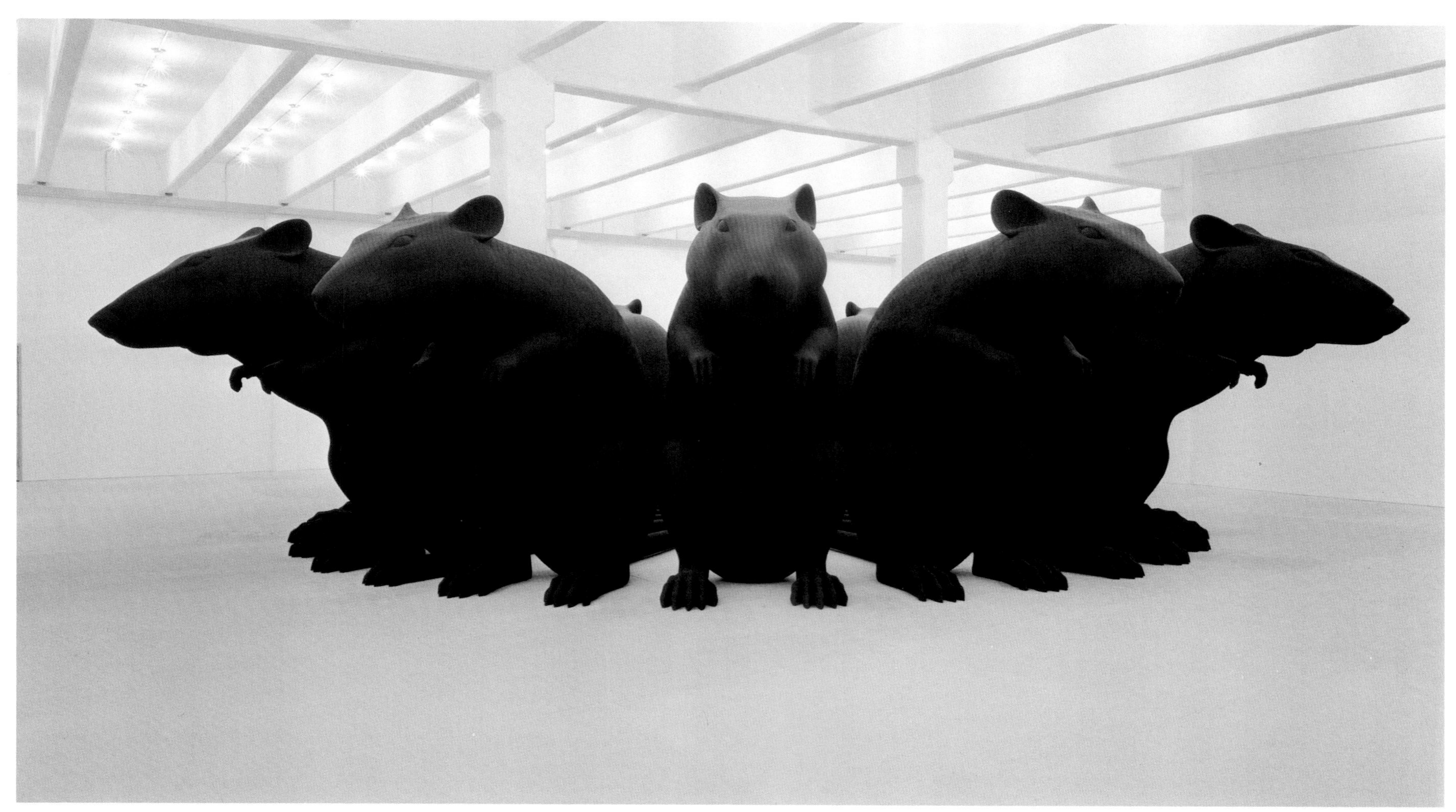

Rattenkönig
1993, Polyester resin, height 110 1/4 inches x diameter 511 3/4 inches

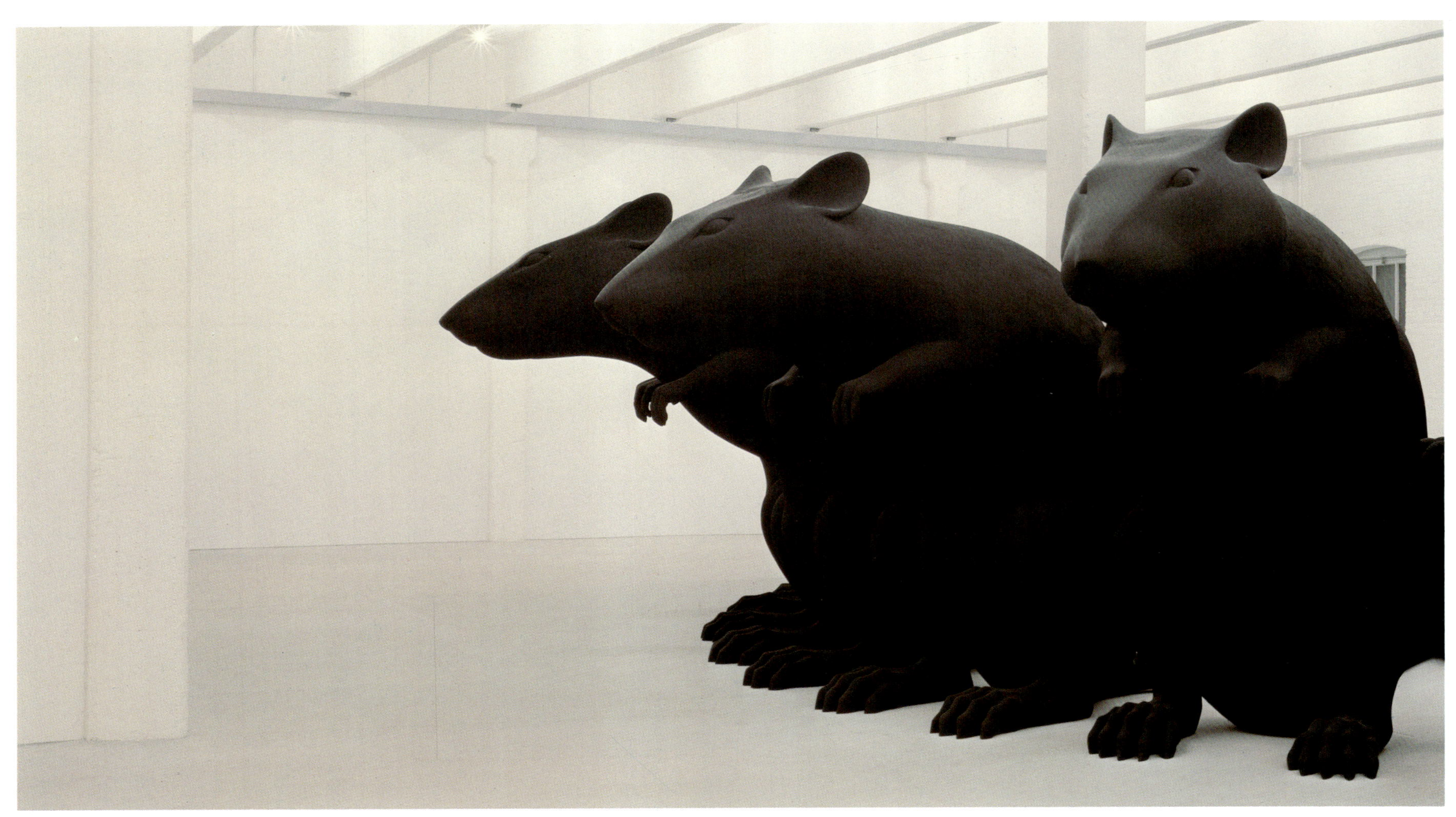

Rattenkönig
1993, Polyester resin, height 110 1/4 inches x diameter 511 3/4 inches

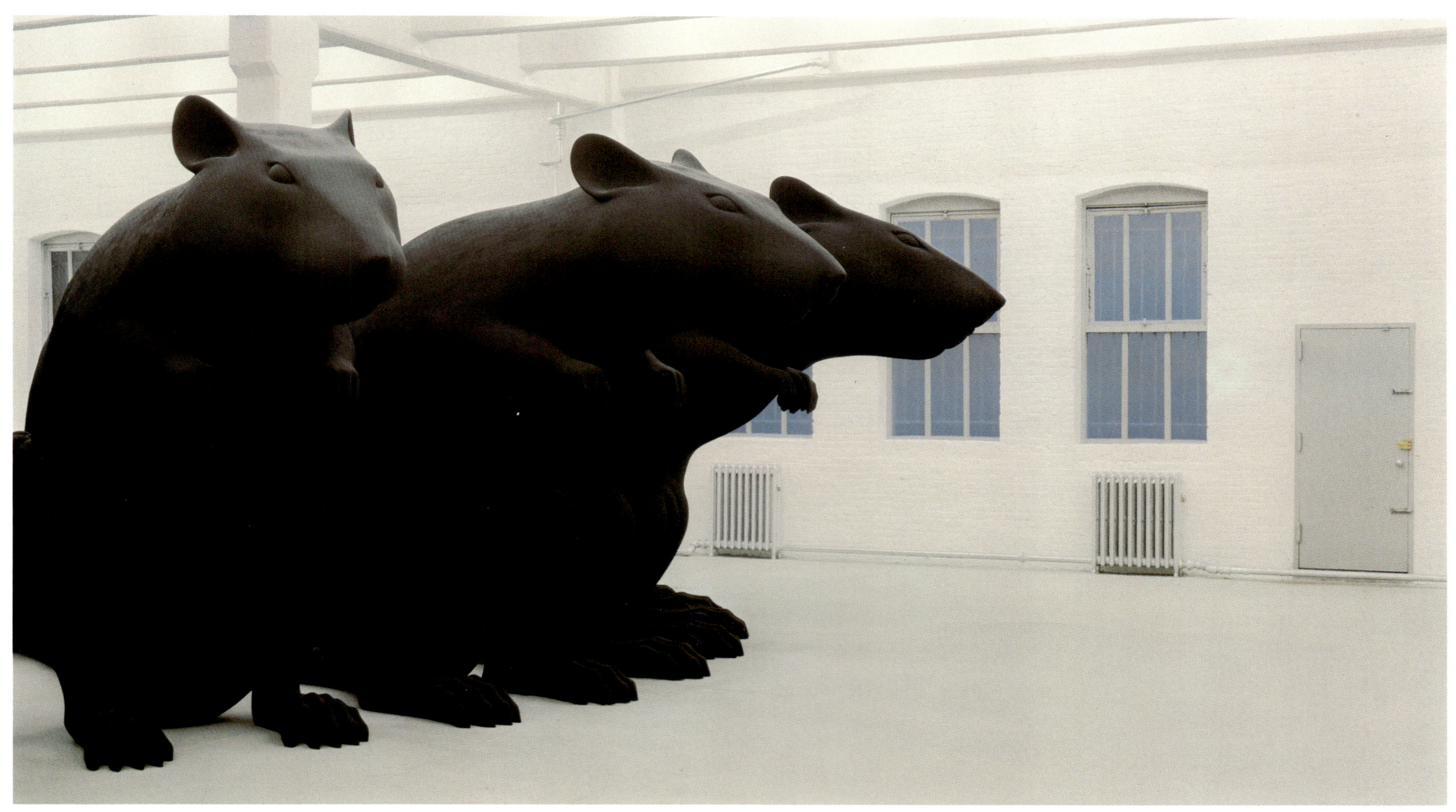

Rattenkönig
1993, Polyester resin, height 110 1/4 inches x diameter 511 3/4 inches

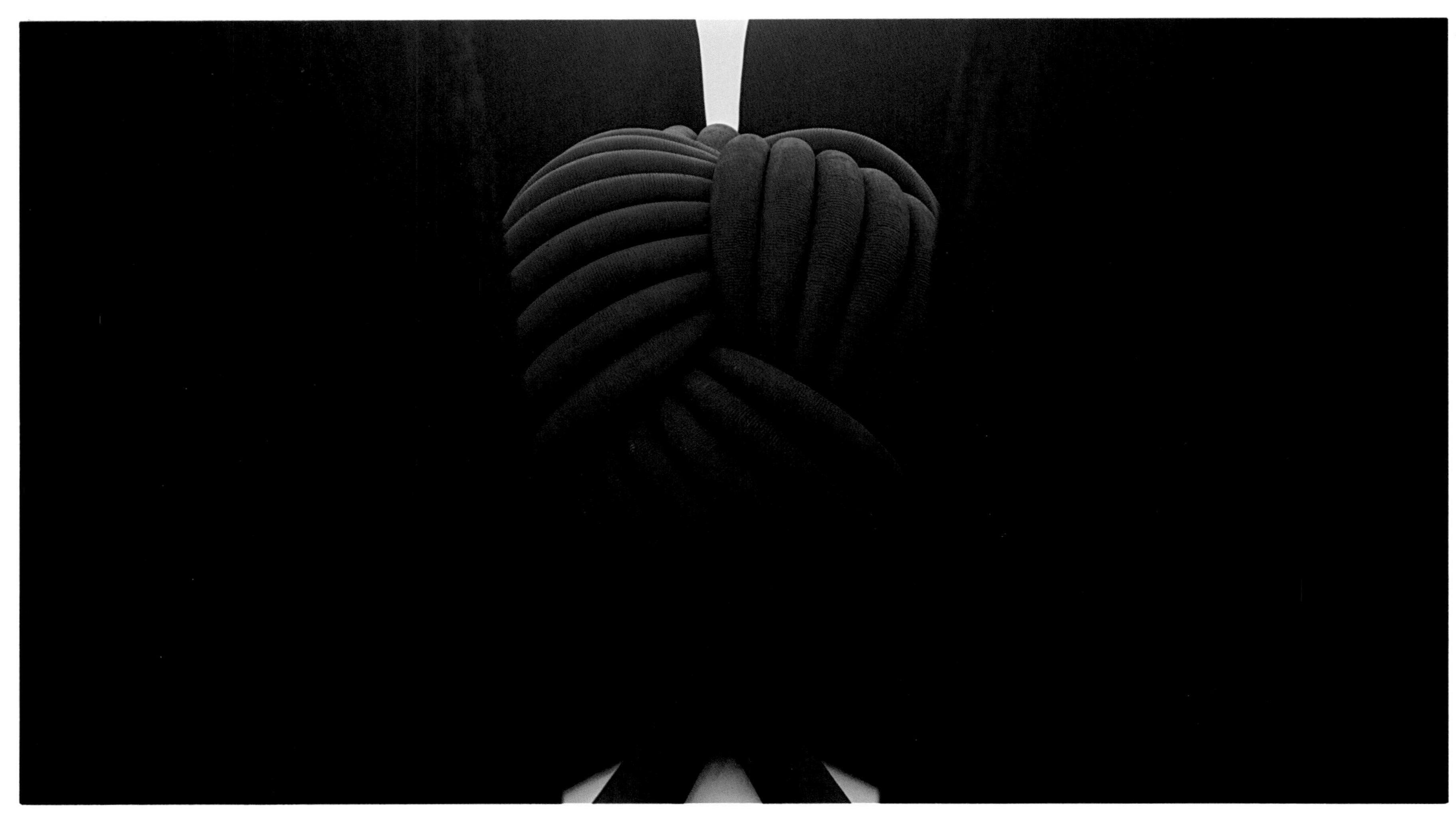

Rattenkönig
1993, Polyester resin, height 110 1/4 inches x diameter 511 3/4 inches

I've Been to New York

In the vast Atlantic, between Europe and what we call the new continent, there is a liquid border. There the waves bubble, the water is warm and sudsy, and vapors and a humid warmth envelop the great ships which roll and pitch among the phantoms of the caravels and the sea creatures emerging from the water, their mouths open, pursuing an imaginary prey. This is the Gulf Stream. A passenger coming from any point in Europe still breathed the air of the Old Country, so to speak. Once this border has been crossed, one is on the other side. Whether one is better or worse off there I do not know. What I do know is that one is in another world. In some imperceptible fashion everything has changed. One feels a bit as if one were dead. Naturally, one still moves. One eats, smokes, walks, talks, reads, or does everything as before, but in all this there is something phantomlike about the activity.

Everything that appears to one arriving in New York—the skyscrapers on Wall Street, the fog, the tug boats, that whole elongated architecture, white, cubist, and neatly arranged, which makes you think of historical reconstructions of Babylon and imperial Rome done in plaster from conscientious plans and archaeologists' drawings—is bathed in an otherworldly light.

America has already existed as America for a few centuries. Great cities have been built, and a reflective and hardworking people has developed, and endlessly continues to develop, there. It thus seems something of an exaggeration to still call it the New World. It is no longer a new world, but it surely is and always will be another world. This is not merely a question of civilization, mentality, mores, or of some social, economic, or mechanical progress more or less ahead of Europe. It's rather a question of molecules, climate, different air, or a special quality of the sun's rays. The light and temperature are different. There is something of the humid warmth of a hothouse, even in the middle of winter; there is also a hothouse light. In America, human and object lose their shadow. There is also a strange softness; everything is more tender and as if made of the same matter. The bones of human and animal, and stones and metals, seem less hard than in Europe; everything seems less dry and less hard than in Europe. That explains the strange sheen that flowers, fruit, vegetables, and women's skin have in America. The slight flaw which weighs on everything is also an otherworldly flaw.

European from old Europe, if you can, go visit New York; go visit that city of fever and dream. You will discover strange beauties and see apparitions which have absolutely nothing in common with anything cinema has shown and literature has written about that country until now. Behind the barrier of the Ocean, beyond customs and the Irish with their black-waxed revolvers, behind the white-gloved phantoms who unload debris from the seven sins into armored cars in the light of pallid dawns, you will find, again and again, in New York the Magnificent, New York the Eternal New, forgotten memories which return there as they return in the hours of semi-sleep, those mysterious hours when soul and spirit, finally disengaged from logic and reality, solve a throng of otherwise insoluble enigmas and problems—alas, forgotten as soon as they are solved. In an apotheosis of fireworks, luxury and richness create in this mysterious new New York these strange paradises in the very center of this immense and ancient city, mechanical and polymorphous, paradises which transport us at a soft and imperceptible speed, with no jolts or jerks, in padded sleighs drawn by polychromed ducks and the good storks from our memories of yesteryear….

Splendid city of dreams within a dream, city of shop windows, Shop Window City, Storefront City: through its windows parade, day and night, like the figures of a very old clock, all the things of dim humanity, from its remote cradle drowned in the mists of sylvan and cavernous paleontology to the spectacular and electric aspects of its dark future. New York, the Eternal New, draws us along its infinite parallels, into the implausible kaleidoscope of its storefronts, transparent towers, splendid bazaars, and shop windows lit through the long winter nights—where the ineffable Dioscuri sleep, leaning up against the breastplates of their tired horses, and the characters in Meyerling's drama consult their watchdials and, without seeing them, lean over their rusty spyglasses and sabers, which once were clutched in the tight fists of one-eyed buccaneers, now long dead. In this forest of glass, steel, and cement, in this extraordinary New York difficult to define, you will find, O Traveler, the gigantic masks of ancient gods. You will find the eternal sadness of plaster busts of Antinous and the immense solitude of the Parthenon in the summer nights, under the great sky streaming with stars.

Giorgio de Chirico, Paris, January 29, 1938

Katharina Fritsch

List of Illustrated Works

<u>Tischgesellschaft</u>
Company at Table, 1988
Polyester, wood, and cotton, 55 x 630 x 69 in. (140 x 1600 x 175 cm.)
Museum für Moderne Kunst, Frankfurt am Main, Germany
Dauerleihgabe Dresdner Bank, Frankfurt am Main, Germany

<u>Mann und Maus</u>
Man and Mouse, 1992, edition of 2
Polyester resin, 90 1/2 x 51 1/5 x 94 1/2 in. (230 x 130 x 270 cm.)
Collection of Simone Ackermans, Germany
Private Collection, United States

<u>Rattenkönig</u>
Rat-King, 1993
Polyester resin, H: 110 1/4 in. x Diam. 511 3/4 in. (2.8 m x 13 m.)
Courtesy Katharina Fritsch

Biography

lives and works in Düsseldorf

1956   born in Essen

1977   Kunstakademie, Düsseldorf

1981   advanced studies (<u>Meisterschüler</u>) with Professor Fritz Schwegler

Individual Exhibitions

1984   Galerie Rüdiger Schöttle, Munich (with Thomas Ruff)

1985   Galerie Johnen & Schöttle, Cologne
        Galerie Schneider, Konstanz (with Thomas Ruff and Bernd Jünger)

1987   Kaiser Wilhelm Museum, Krefeld

1988   Kunsthalle, Basel
        Institute of Contemporary Art, London

1989   Kunstverein, Münster
        Portikus, Frankfurt

1990   Galerie Rüdiger Schöttle, Munich

1993   Dia Center for the Arts, New York

Group Exhibitions

1982   <u>Möbel perdu</u>, Museum für Kunst und Gewerbe, Hamburg
        Galerie B14, Stuttgart
        <u>(ORTE) DER ZEHN HEILIGEN GELIEBTEN</u>, Galerie
        Schloss Hardenberg, Velbert-Neviges

1984   <u>von hier aus</u>, Messegelände Halle 13, Düsseldorf

1986   <u>von Raum zu Raum</u>, Kunstverein, Hamburg
        <u>Sonsbeek '86</u>, Arnhem
        <u>Aus den Anfängen</u>, Kunstfonds, Bonn
        <u>Europa/Amerika</u>, Museum Ludwig, Cologne
        <u>Junge Rheinische Kunst</u>, Galerie Schipka, Sofia
        <u>A Distanced View</u>, The New Museum of Contemporary Art,
        New York

1987   <u>Anderer Leute Kunst</u>, Museum Haus Lange, Krefeld
        <u>Skulptur Projekte Münster</u>, Münster
        <u>Bestiarum</u>, Galerie Rüdiger Schöttle, Munich
        <u>Multiples</u>, Galerie Daniel Buchholz, Cologne
        Ydessa Gallery, Toronto

1988   <u>Cultural Geometry</u>, Deste Foundation for Contemporary Art, House of Cyprus, Athens
<u>Collections pour une région</u>, Musée d'Art Contemporain, Bordeaux
Galerie Johnen & Schöttle, Cologne
<u>Biennale of Sydney</u>, Sydney
<u>BiNATIONALE: German Art of the late '80s</u>, Institute of Contemporary Art, Boston; Museum of Fine Arts, Boston
<u>Carnegie International</u>, Carnegie Institute, Pittsburgh

1989   Stichting De Appel, Amsterdam
<u>What is Contemporary Art</u>? Rooseum, Malmö
<u>Mondi Possibili</u>, Galerie Monika Sprüth, Cologne
Galerie Ghislaine Hussenot, Paris

1990   <u>New Work: A New Generation</u>, San Francisco Museum of Modern Art, San Francisco
<u>Culture and Commentary: An Eighties Perspective</u>, Hirshhorn Museum and Sculpture Garden, Smithsonian Institution, Washington, D.C.
<u>Weitersehen 1980–1990</u>, Museum Haus Esters/Haus Lange, Krefeld
<u>Hanne Darboven, Walter Dahn, Katharina Fritsch, Reinhard Mucha, Rosemarie Trockel</u>, Barbara Gladstone Gallery, New York
<u>OBJECTives: The New Sculpture</u>, Newport Harbor Museum, Newport Beach
<u>Semi-Objects</u>, John Good Gallery, New York
<u>Color and/or Monochrome</u>, National Museum of Modern Art, Tokyo

1991   <u>Metropolis</u>, Martin Gropius-Bau, Berlin
<u>Carnegie International 1991</u>, Carnegie Institute, Pittsburgh
<u>In anderen Räumen</u>, Museum Haus Esters/Haus Lange, Krefeld
<u>Standpunkt der Moderne. Von Picasso bis Clemente: Werke aus der Emanuel Hoffmann-Stiftung Basel</u>, Deichtorhallen, Hamburg
Luhring Augustine Gallery, New York
Galerie Locus Solus, Genoa

<u>Contemporary Art from the Collection of Jason Rubell</u>, Duke University Museum of Art, Durham, North Carolina
<u>L'espai i la idea. Selecció d'obres de la collecció d'art contemporani Fundació "la Caixa</u>," Barcelona (traveling extensively 1989–1993)

1992   <u>Doubletake: Collective Memory & Current Art</u>, Hayward Gallery, London
<u>7: Thomas Bernstein, Günther Förg, Katharina Fritsch, Isa Genzken, Hubert Kiecol, Wilhelm Mundt, Thomas Schütte</u>, Galeria Zacheta, Warsaw
<u>Der Teppich des Lebens</u>, Haus Koekkoek, Kleve
<u>Oh! Cet écho!</u> Centre Culturel Suisse, Paris
<u>Ars Pro Domo: Contemporary Art from Cologne Private Collections</u>, Museum Ludwig, Cologne

1993   <u>Doubletake: Kollektives Gedächtnis & Heutige Kunst</u>, Kunsthalle, Vienna

Bibliography

1981   Fritsch, Katharina. <u>Werbeblatt</u> 1. Düsseldorf, 1981.

1983   Fritsch, Katharina. "Friedhöfe," <u>Kunstforum International</u>, no. 65 (September 1983), 74–75.

1984   Kraft, Monika M. "Katharina Fritsch," <u>von hier aus</u>. Exhibition catalogue. Düsseldorf: Messegelände Halle 13 (1984), 280–283.

1986   Bos, Saskia and Jan Brand. "Katharina Fritsch," <u>Sonsbeek '86</u>. Exhibition catalogue. Arnhem (1986), 186–187.

Gumpert, Lynn. "A Distanced View," <u>Zien</u>, no. 9 (1986), 6–12.

Jochimsen, M. "Alles hat seine Vorgeschichte," <u>Junge Rheinische Kunst</u>. Exhibition catalogue. Sofia: Galerie Schipka (1986), 13–23.

Locker, Ludwig. "Architektonische Aspekte in der Düsseldorfer Gegenwartskunst," Artefactum 2, no. 12 (February–March 1986), 2–9.

Messler, Norbert. "Raum und Bildwelt," von Raum zu Raum. Exhibition catalogue. Hamburg: Kunstverein Hamburg (1986), 23–24.

1987   Blase, Christoph. "Ein normaler Elefant und anderes Greifbares," Kunst Plus Kunst (1987), 54–55.

Cameron, Dan. "The Critic's Way," Artforum XXVI, no. 1 (September 1987), 119.

Galloway, David. "Report from Germany," Art in America 75, no. 12 (December 1987), 21.

Heartney, Eleanor. "Sighted in Münster," Art in America 75, no. 9 (September 1987), 140–143.

Hermes, Manfred. "Katharina Fritsch at the Kaiser Wilhelm Museum, Krefeld," Flash Art 137 (November–December 1987), 112–113.

Heynen, Julian. "Anbieten/Aufhaben/Grün-Elefant-Erscheinen/Verschwinden," Katharina Fritsch—Elefant. Exhibition catalogue. Krefeld: Kaiser Wilhelm Museum (1987).

Heynen, Julian. "Other People's Art," Anderer Leute Kunst. Exhibition catalogue. Krefeld: Museum Haus Lange (1987), 6–10.

Koether, Jutta. "Elephant," Parkett 13 (1987), 90–92.

Ponti, L.L. "Il progetto scultura a Münster," Domus, no. 686 (September 1987), 110–111.

Puvogel, Renate. "Katharina Fritsch: Elefant," Kunstforum International, no. 89 (May–June 1987), 338–340.

Schmidt-Wulffen, Stephan. "Enzyklopädie der Skulptur," Kunstforum International, no. 91 (October–November 1987), 288–301.

Wilmers, Ulrich. "Madonna," Skulptur Projekte Münster 1987. Exhibition catalogue. Münster: Westfälisches Landesmuseum für Kunst und Kulturgeschichte (1987), 89–92.

1988   Ammann, Jean-Christophe. "The Intuitive Logic of Katharina Fritsch," Katharina Fritsch. Exhibition catalogue. Kunsthalle Basel/ICA London (1988), 7–9.

Archer, Michael. "Rosemarie Trockel and Katharina Fritsch," Art Monthly, no. 121 (November 1988), 20–21

Beyer, Lucie and Karen Marta. "Report From Germany: Why Cologne?" Art in America 76, no. 12 (December 1988), 45–51.

Blase, Christoph. "Katharina Fritsch: Ich wäre gerne eine Firma," VOGUE Deutschland (June 1988), 78–80.

Blase, Christoph. "On Katharina Fritsch," Artscribe 68 (March–April 1988), 52–55.

Christov-Bakargiev, Carolyn. "Something Nowhere," Flash Art 140 (May–June 1988), 80–85.

Godfrey, Tony. "Report From Germany: A Tale of Four Cities," Art in America 76, no. 11 (November 1988), 33–41.

Krebs, Edith. "Katharina Fritsch/Rosemarie Trockel," NOEMA, no. 20 (September–October 1988), 79.

Koether, Jutta. "A Report from the Field (A Question of Physical Presence)," Flash Art 141 (Summer 1988), 87–89.

Puvogel, Renate. "Katharina Fritsch, Rosemarie Trockel, Anna Winteler," Kunstforum International, no. 97 (November–December 1988), 313–317.

Salvioni, Daniela. "Trockel and Fritsch, Kunsthalle, Basel," Flash Art 142 (October 1988), 110.

Syring, Marie Luise and Christiane Vielhaber. "Interview with Katharina Fritsch," BiNATIONALE: German Art of the Late '80s. Exhibition catalogue. Düsseldorf: Städtische Kunsthalle (1988), 116–121.

1989   Beyer, Lucie. "Katharina Fritsch: Kunstverein, Münster/Portikus, Frankfurt," Arena, no. 4 (October 1989), 99–100.

Blase, Christoph. "Die Kunst mit den reproduzierenden Medien," Artis (September 1989), 54–57.

Cameron, Dan. "How We Have Changed, Revisited," Arena, no. 1 (February 1989), 70.

Cottingham, Laura. "The Feminine De-Mystique," Flash Art 147 (Summer 1989), 91–95.

Koether, Jutta. "Katharina Fritsch: Kunstverein, Münster/Portikus, Frankfurt," Artscribe 78 (November–December 1989), 85–86.

Heymer, Kay. "Alles Gleichzeitig," Bremer Kunstpreis 1989, Bremen: Bremen Kunsthalle, 29–35.

Heynen, Julian. "Familiarity—Alienation—Realization," Katharina Fritsch 1979–1989. Münster: Westfälischer Kunstverein/Frankfurt am Main: Portikus (1989), 67–71.

Magnani, Gregorio. "This Is Not Conceptual," Flash Art 145 (March–April 1989), 84–87.

Messler, Norbert. "Ordnungstrieb und Präzision," Wolkenkratzer, no. 5 (September–October 1989), 80–81.

Messler, Norbert. "Katharina Fritsch at Kunstverein, Münster," Artforum XXVIII, no. 2 (October 1989), 189.

Reust, Hans-Rudolf. "Rosemarie Trockel—Katharina Fritsch," Artscribe 73 (January–February 1989), 88–89.

Smolik, Noemi. "Katharina Fritsch, Portikus, Frankfurt," NOEMA, no. 27 (November–December 1989), 97.

Spector, Nancy. "Carnegie International," Contemporanea 5 (February 1989), 104–105.

Stecker, Raimund. "Über junge Düsseldorfer Künstler," Das Kunstwerk 4-5 XLI (January 1989), 129–147.

Suermann, Marie-Theres. "Katharina Fritsch," Contemporanea 13 (December 1989), 51–54.

1990   New Work: A New Generation. Exhibition catalogue. San Francisco: San Francisco Museum of Modern Art (1990).

Weitersehen 1980–1990. Exhibition catalogue. Krefeld: Museum Haus Esters/Haus Lange (1990), 195–199. Texts by Stephan Schmidt-Wulffen, Juan Muñoz, Alain Cueff, Hannes Böhringer.

Cameron, Dan. "Setting Standards," Parkett 25 (1990), 64–73.

Garrels, Gary. "Disarming Perception," Parkett 25 (1990), 36–43.

Halbreich, Kathy. "Katharina Fritsch," <u>Culture and Commentary: An Eighties Perspective</u>. Exhibition catalogue. Washington D.C.: Hirshhorn Museum and Sculpture Garden, Smithsonian Institution (1990), 56–61.

Heynen, Julian. "Speculation on Trucks, Cemeteries, Foxes and Other Images," <u>Parkett</u> 25 (1990), 53–63.

Kuoni, Carin. "Kultur und Kommentar, ein Ansatz der achtziger Jahre," <u>Kunst-Bulletin</u>, no. 7/8 (July–August 1990), 28–35.

Schloss, C. "Katharina Fritsch," <u>Juliet</u> (April 1990), 30.

Schmidt-Wulffen, Stephan. "Katharina Fritsch: Mechanisms of Epiphany," <u>OBJECTives: The New Sculpture</u>. Exhibition catalogue. Newport Beach: Newport Harbor Art Museum (1990), 48–52.

1991   <u>Contemporary Art from the Collection of Jason Rubell</u>. Exhibition catalogue. Durham: Duke University Museum of Art (1991), 28–29.

Vischer, Theodora. "Katharina Fritsch," <u>Emanuel Hoffmann-Stiftung Basel</u>. Exhibition catalogue. Basel (1991), 201–205.

Cooke, Lynne. "Katharina Fritsch," <u>Carnegie International 1991</u>. Exhibition catalogue. Pittsburgh: Carnegie International (1991), 74–75.

1992   <u>TROPISMES. Collección Fundació "la Caixa."</u> Exhibition catalogue. Barcelona: Centre Cultural de la Fundació Caixa de Pensions (1992).

Cooke, Lynne. "The Site of Memory," <u>Doubletake: Collective Memory and Current Art</u>. Exhibition catalogue. London: Hayward Gallery/ Vienna: Kunsthalle (1992), 23–39.

Deitcher, David. "Art on the Installation Plan: MoMA and the Carnegie," <u>Artforum</u> XXX, no. 5 (January 1992), 78–84.

Faust, Gretchen. "Katharina Fritsch at Luhring Augustine Gallery," <u>Arts Magazine</u> 66, no. 5 (January 1992), 84–87.

Heynen, Julian. "Katharina Fritsch—Mann und Maus," <u>7: Thomas Bernstein, Günther Förg, Katharina Fritsch, Isa Genzken, Hubert Kiecol, Wilhelm Mundt, Thomas Schütte</u>. Exhibition catalogue. Warsaw: Galeria Zacheta (1992), 23–29.

Lillington, David. "Always on My Mind …," <u>Frieze</u> 4 (April–May 1992), 12–13.

Morgan, Stuart. "Thanks for the Memories," <u>Frieze</u> 4 (April–May 1992), 6–11.

Wulffen, Thomas. "Red Box—über Katharina Fritschs 'Roter Raum mit Kamingeräusch,'" <u>Meta</u> (1992), 34–36.

Acknowledgments

Katharina Fritsch has worked on <u>Rattenkönig</u> (Rat-King) for over two years now, almost to the exclusion of other work. Her singlemindedness and dedication have been an inspiration to us and the many individuals who have been involved in the project.

In the manufacture of the work itself, we owe a great debt of thanks to Bernhard Kucken, who worked with Katharina to shape the plaster positive (from which the molds were made) of the sculptural form. Christine Lidrbauch and Charles Bills made revisions to the knot form working with Katharina long hours virtually to the last day to finalize the form.

Jim Schaeufele, Director of Operations on Dia's staff, played a critical role in working with Katharina to organize the extensive work here in New York over several months to complete and install the work. Gary Garrels, now at the Walker Art Center, began the project with me before moving to Minneapolis, and since then Lynne Cooke, curator at Dia, has been an invaluable partner in the project. Karen Kelly has overseen the production of the catalogue, with assistance from Sara Schnittjer, Anastasia Aukeman, Marion Delhees, and Brigitte Kölle. I would also like to thank Lynne Cooke and Dr. Christian Winter for their helpful texts.

Finally, we would like to acknowledge major funding received from the National Endowment for the Arts, with additional support from The Cowles Charitable Trust; the Institut für Auslandsbeziehungen; the Dia Art Council, the major annual support group of the Dia Center for the Arts; and the Dia Art Circle. International transportation was provided by Lufthansa German Airlines. Support for the 1992–93 exhibitions program has been provided through a generous grant from The Andy Warhol Foundation for the Visual Arts, Inc.

Charles Wright
Executive Director

Katharina Fritsch

Rattenkönig (Rat-King)

April 1993–April 1994
Dia Center for the Arts
548 West 22nd Street, New York City

Library of Congress Catalogue Card Number: 93-71631
ISBN 0-944521-26-6

Copyright © Dia Center for the Arts and Katharina Fritsch

Texts by Christian Winter and Giorgio de Chirico selected by Katharina Fritsch. "I've Been to New York" by Giorgio de Chirico was translated by Warren Niesluchowski for this publication. It was originally published in French as "J'ai été à New York" in Il meccanismo del pensiero: Critica, polemica, autobiografia 1911–1943 by Giorgio de Chirico, edited by Maurizio Fagiolo. Copyright © 1985 Giulio Einaudi editore s.p.a. Torino.

Publication Coordination by Karen Kelly.
Design by Katharina Fritsch with Karen Kelly and Marion Delhees.
Printed by The Studley Press, Dalton, Massachusetts.

Photograph on page 15 by Frank Fenstermacher. Photographs on pages 16 and 17 by Nic Tenwiggenhorn. Photographs on pages 19-22 by Bill Jacobson Studio, New York.